Passport to Walking by the spirit

Or the Journey of Indeed

Mikaël Réale

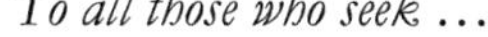
To all those who seek …

FSC
www.fsc.org
MIXTE
Papier issu
de sources
responsables
Paper from
responsible sources
FSC® C105338

Édition: BoD – Books on Demand, info@bod.fr
Printed by BoD – Books on Demand, In de Tarpen 42, Norderstedt (Allemagne)
Print on demand
Legal Deposit: March 2024
ISBN: 978-2-3225-2318-4
First published: March 2024

Foreword

For as long as I can remember, I've loved traveling. When I was a child, my friends wanted to become policemen, firemen or do what Dad was doing, but I wanted to be a seaman in the merchant navy!

At the age of 9, I had my first opportunity to get on a sailboat, and it was a revelation. I was made for it and that's what I hoped to do with my life. When I was 16, I met a French singer, writer and sailor, Antoine, in Tahiti. I had already read his book "Bord à bord" and he had become my hero. I went on to devour all his books. Two months later, while running away from a violent father, I secretly boarded a French cargo ship in the port of Papeete, the Cézanne, on which I traveled 1,250 kilometers to Mururoa atoll before being sent home to my parents in an air force plane.

In the years that followed, I traveled alone, hitchhiking, flying and sailing. Earning a living along the way playing guitar in cafés and restaurants, I crossed all of Europe, then the USA and finally the South Pacific on a 14-meter sailboat. After many adventures and misadventures, it was in New Zealand that God caught up with me in 1984. (The full story is in Mikael's book: Chased by Your Grace).

So it was quite natural that, in 1986, after getting married, Cathy and I set off across the Caribbean on a sailboat we'd bought in Martinique. I couldn't see my life any other way than traveling, and preferably on a sailboat! I refused to be one of those sedentary landlubbers stuck in a normal lifestyle!

However, one day in the summer of 1987, while Cathy and I were in northern Quebec, I realized the price Christ had paid on the cross, and I gave my life entirely to him, rather than inviting him to participate when I needed or wanted Him to. I had understood and accepted that God wanted me to entrust my destiny to Him, and to do so, He was asking me to offer Him my love of the sea and travel as a sacrifice.

This was surely the hardest thing in my life to give up! Although I agreed to obey immediately, it actually took me more than three years to truly let go of it in both my heart and my mind. But finally, I woke up one morning with a passion far stronger than that of the sea. I was simply passionate about the Kingdom of God!

Cathy and I decided to go to Bible College together and serve God full-time. We had two little boys and the idea of opening a shelter for drug addicts in Savoie. I was trained as a drug prevention worker, but we wanted to combine this with biblical training to anchor the project in a spiritual framework.

So it was with great surprise that in 1990, at a Christian convention, I realized that God wanted to send me into the mission field. At first, I didn't believe it and even resisted the idea. Wasn't the devil trying to make me give up my good resolutions? Hadn't I obeyed God by giving up my life of travel?

It was only five years later, as part of the ministry in which I was engaged, that I left with my wife and three children for the island of Madagascar.

A few months before our departure, in February 1995, when I had decided to spend a week in fasting and prayer, a team-mate came to pray with me. God's presence was particularly evident that day, and I was soon given a prophetic word: "Since you trusted me and agreed to sacrifice your Isaac to me, I'll give him back to you one day, and you'll serve me with him. Then the brother added: "I see you on a sailboat, traveling to bring the Kingdom to the nations. I don't know if this is important, but I see that it's a boat, with the aft mast higher than the foremast"...

This detail, which may seem insignificant, was not. A few years earlier, while sailing across the South Pacific, I had drawn the sailboat I'd dreamed of building for myself. It was a schooner, with the aft mast higher than the foremast... It was like a wink from God, telling me: "you see, this is me talking to you".

However, I had so surrendered my passion for sailing and travel to God that this revelation was greeted with faith, certainly, but without any excitement. I couldn't make the connection between sailing and ministry. For me, ministry had taken on far more interest than my former passion. I put this aside for the next 5 years.

For our wedding anniversary in 2000, we took a few days' vacation from Reunion Island to Mauritius. People from the congregation looked after the children for us, and those four days did us a lot of good. One evening, as we were walking along the seafront, I saw a sailboat at anchor and it was like a revelation. I could now, make the connection between God's promise to give me a sailboat and the ministry for which I had given my life.

At that time, I already felt cramped in the ministry of a local church, but I couldn't see myself traveling and living out of a pair of suitcases as an on-the-go minister. Besides, I like to build relationships by taking my time with people. That's hardly possible when you spend two days visiting a church you won't see again for months or years.

But a boat was like a house that would follow us, allowing us to be at home while traveling, and so be able to spend weeks, even months, in one place, working for the Kingdom of God, without being completely uprooted each time.

But even though I could now understand the potential of a boat in my ministry, we had three children between the ages of 7 and 12, and I couldn't see myself taking them on this kind of journey.

Two years later, after some difficult times in our mission work, God granted us a sabbatical in England. We were in a process of restoration, and the very thought of ministry had drifted far from my daily life. Despite this, one evening in a house meeting, two people gave us prophetic words.

The first was that God had led us into a sheltered bay after a storm to restore our sails and rigging. God would then send us back to the mission...

The second said: "Mikael and Cathy, God has anointed you for the islands, and you have received this call to respond to Isaiah's verse 'For the islands hope in me, and the ships of Tarsis are in the lead, to bring back your children from afar'. This is your mission field. This is where you must go!

We did indeed go on mission again, but not to the islands. Two years in the USA was not a very pleasant time, in fact, and there is much to say about it - we'll come back to that later.

Then we returned to France, and planted a church in Toulon, where we served until 2015.

After several years, we were exhausted and disillusioned by this pastoral work. Cathy and I felt that we had come to the end of a season, and that we would soon have to leave again. In January, as we had done every year for 2 decades, we undertook a Daniel fast in order to hear and understand God's will for the new year.

At the end of this fast, God reactivated the prophecy I had received 20 years earlier concerning the sailboat! My son Maël's wife, who lives in Australia, had called us and said: *'Dad, it's time to go! And God is going to give you a sailboat for it'.*

I was overcome by a wave of joy and faith! We felt that not only were we entering a new season, for our life, our ministry... but that the word about the sailboat given 20 years earlier was now coming true.

As a friend with whom I shared this project remarked at the time: 'It's a new season for the Church and for those who serve God. When I think of you, I always have one small regret: you're too sedentary. But you're an adventurer! Secondly, lots of ministries are going to be really "out of the box" in these new times. They're going to do it in relation to who they really are, not in accordance with the mold they're being pressed into'.

As I listened to him, I realized that this project was really us! We were called to it, we were gifted for it, and we had offered our lives to God for it! 'Delight yourself in the Lord... And He will give you what your heart desires'.

It was clear that, as usual, we were ready to drop everything to follow the Lord!

But to do what? And how?

'Indeed'

When my daughter-in-law in Australia gave us this word, I laughed and felt like Sarah when she heard the announcement of her future pregnancy. "A sailboat? But... I can't anymore... and for what? Anyway, we didn't have a penny. I quickly checked our bank account and realized the obvious: I had the sum of 47 euros available!

Since our departure for Madagascar in 1995, Cathy and I had decided never to be in debt again. A loan was not an option for the purchase of a sailboat.

However, as time went by, we became more and more convinced that we were facing our destiny in Christ. So we started looking for a sailboat.

A few days later, while looking at ads on a specialized website, I spotted a 9-meter sailboat that wasn't very expensive. I called and made an appointment for the following Sunday.

Cathy and I were convinced at first glance that this was the one to buy. When we got home, we decided to make an offer, even though we didn't have the first penny for it.

If, despite being well below the asking price, it was accepted, we would assume we were on the right track… And our offer was accepted! All that remained was to find the financing before the following Saturday, when we were due to meet for the transaction.

On Thursday afternoon, just as I was despairing of finding a solution, I received a call from a friend who asked me: "You don't happen to have a new project on the go, do you? I'd like to finance it to a certain level".

As it happened, he covered the offer we had made to the seller. By Saturday, we owned "Indeed", our new sailboat.

In the months that followed, for every expense, planned or unforeseen, to restore the boat, and then to undertake the voyage, it was provided for in the same miraculous way.

I'm not going to list all the financial and other miracles we saw during those times, because the list would be too long, and that's not the point.

But one thing is certain, as a friend of mine used to say: "When God sends, He provides"!

"The desire and the Power"

For God is working in you, giving you the desire and the power to do what pleases him. [1]

So, now what do you do with a 30-foot boat?

I've always had a tendency to put my "two cents" into God's plans, and I'm sure I'm not the only one. However, in some people, and in me in particular, this tendency is more developed than in others. So, of course, after the miraculous purchase of the sailboat, I started to make plans!

For several days, something had been running through my mind as I prayed. "Start with Israel". But I couldn't see the point of heading east with the sailboat.

One place, however, particularly appealed to me because I knew I could do a lot there, both in the humanitarian and evangelical fields: Haiti.

Several months earlier, I had received an invitation to preach in a Haitian church in the Dominican Republic, the Spanish-speaking part of the island. So I went there with the intention of checking out mission possibilities for us.

I was on a bus to a small town on the south coast of the island, to check on the formalities for coming with the boat and sailing between Haiti and Dominica.

[1] Philippians 2:13

I then clearly felt a question formulating in my heart. Did I want to continue planning and organizing my trip... or did I want to walk in God's miraculous plans? Lord, I want to walk with you!" I said spontaneously.

At that moment I was seized with an intense, supernatural joy. I was laughing inside! This lasted until the bus arrived in the town I was going to.

Then, as I got out of the bus, I saw a flagpole in the middle of the square, with the flag of... Israel flying at the top!

Perhaps there was a rational reason for the flag of Israel to be flying in the central square of a small town in the Dominican Republic - there certainly was! But for me it was a genuine sign that God was sending me.

When I returned to France 10 days later, I was convinced. Before going anywhere, we'd start by taking our boat to Israel. To do what? I still didn't know, but God would tell me in time!

Cathy was particularly happy about this change of plan, as she couldn't see herself crossing the Atlantic on a 30-foot sailboat.

A friend, in charge of our church group, was also convinced that this was what God wanted from us.

The more we shared this project with people, the more a general idea emerged. It was as if with every conversation, God was adding a piece to the puzzle through the people we were talking to. Some had an idea, others a word, others asked us: "What if you visited so-and-so in Jericho, so-and-so in Tel Aviv...".

Little by little, a plan took shape in our hearts: just like the apostle Paul, we were to make an offering from the church of the nations to the Messianic church in Israel.

Insights, opportunities...
And sometimes revelations!

Many people believe that if a three-meter-high angel with golden wings doesn't appear before them, then God's will isn't being expressed. Yet we can see in the Bible that God sometimes speaks in a storm, sometimes in a soft whisper, and sometimes even in silence.

Insights:

"It seemed good to me…"

In evangelical circles, we often hear the expression: "I have it on my heart". I remember one day, when I was a young Christian, I explained to my pastor that I had set my heart on forming a team with the teenagers from the congregation to do street evangelism.

Cathy and I had just finished Bible school and were eager to serve. Then he said to me:

- Another victim of Heart syndrome.

When I looked bewildered, he said:

- Good. I have this on my heart, I have that on my heart, ... With God, you don't have on your heart! You hear his voice and you obey.

I walked away a little sheepish, not knowing what to think, and especially not knowing what to do with my "desire" to serve.

Yet it's interesting to note how Luke introduces his Gospel:

"it seemed good to me also, having followed all things closely for some time past, to write an orderly account for you, most excellent Theophilus, that you may have certainty concerning the things you have been taught. [2]

It would therefore seem that one of the four Gospels was written not on the basis of revelation, but of intuition!

One might imagine that if God had led Luke to write this Gospel account, which is part of the canon of inspired books recognized by the entire Christian world, he must have had "at least" one vision, if not the apparition of an angel.

But no! God inspired Luke with a rather banal intuition. It would be nice if you could summarize my son's life here on earth.

This impression must, of course, have found its way into the Greek doctor's thoughts, and certainly been confirmed by others. Nevertheless, it started out as an idea.

I can sometimes imagine Luke talking to Paul a few days after the shipwreck in Malta.

- You know, Paul, this time we almost didn't make it.

---

[2] (Luke 1 : 3-4).

- C'mon… You're exaggerating, I told you it was going to go well.

- Anyway, it gave me an idea. We shouldn't die without leaving a written record of everything that happened when Jesus was with us here on earth. And then, one day, why not, tell what happened afterwards, with Peter, and also with Stephen, and why not a "saga" of your travels. We could call it the adventures of Paul & Timothy...

- Well, Luke, you're delirious! First of all, the title! Peter and the others won't like it, and anyway, I'm not even sure they read any of the letters I send them!

I know, I know… This is just a silly storytelling.

Initially very simple feelings can turn out to be a directive from the Lord. Would we allow ourselves to believe that Luke, too, was suffering from "Jack's syndrome"?

For much of my Christian life, I've wanted to reject intuitions. Often considering them too carnal, if not "occult", I distrusted them.

Yet sometimes they became so persistent that I could no longer ignore them.

So, of course, you can't just jump in at the first idea that pops into your head. However, over time I've learned to discern which of my thoughts are worthy of interest and to pursue them.

Sometimes this has been the beginning of great adventures with the Lord.

We can see this principle stated in the very definition of the word intuition:

"Direct and immediate knowledge of a truth that presents itself to the mind with the clarity of evidence, serving as a principle and foundation for discursive reasoning."

It's interesting to note what Henri Poincaré said: "It's with logic that we prove, but with intuition that we find".

It seems to me that this is often the way God leads us.

We have the intuition that He wants something from us. From there, we look for "evidence" that our intuition is well-founded.

The danger is that we sometimes set off on an intuition without really having thought through all the aspects. But if we bother to do two or three basic checks, such as:

1. Is it biblical?

2. Does it correspond to what God himself would say?

3. Is it in line with what God has already asked of me?

For point number one, this shouldn't take much time if you're an avid Bible reader.

For the second, it's the same, but requires that your relationship with God enables you to recognize His voice.

"My sheep recognize my voice. I know them, and they follow me. "[3].

Too many people today know a lot about God without really knowing Him intimately. They quickly become "finger pointers" when you tell them about your desire to do your part for God.

Finally, on the third point, I'd like to say that I don't love a weather vane.

So often, when I was a pastor, I saw people who came to see me every other week and systematically started the conversation with a thundering "God told me!"

---

[3] John 10 : 27

The problem was, it seemed that God had changed his mind from one time to the next.

I'm thinking of one man in particular whom God "told" that such and such a girl was the woman destined for him by the Lord, then it was another and then another that he ended up marrying.

Then God would ask him to leave our town for another, then 6 months later He would ask him to return to the starting point, only to send him away again a few months later... and each time he would say: "God told me"!

The problem is, God isn't like that at all. Here's how He defines Himself in His Word

"God is not a man, so he does not lie.

He is not human, so he does not change his mind.

Has he ever spoken and failed to act?

Has he ever promised and not carried it through?" [4]

Likewise, Paul explains: *"For God's gifts and his call can never be withdrawn."*.[5]

Christians need to stop believing that every morning God wakes up, sees you and wonders what he's going to do with you today!

Not only does God have a specific plan for you, but he's given you everything you need to carry it out from the start.

"For I know the plans I have for you," says the LORD. They are plans for good and not for disaster, to give you a future and a hope. ". [6]

---

[4] Numbers 23 : 19

[5] Romans 11 :29

[6] Jeremiah 29 : 11

"I knew you before I formed you in your mother's womb. Before you were born I set you apart and appointed you as my prophet to the nations. ". [7]

There is no randomness with God. Even before the foundation of the world, He had already prepared a plan for the redemption of mankind. He has a plan for every human being - a plan A, a plan B, a plan...

In order to know whether an intuition is from God or not, one of the points that always attracts my attention is the persistence of that intuition.

I have dozens of ideas running through my head every day. They come and go... but sometimes one idea never leaves me. I fall asleep with it at night and wake up with it in the morning!

This often lasts until I decide to pay more attention to it. It's not necessarily an "inspired" idea, but it's worth checking out.

When I was 15, I started teaching sailing at the sailing club where my mother was secretary. I discovered that I had a gift for explaining things to people, and that I actually enjoyed it! A few years later, I was teaching French in New Zealand and enjoying it too.

As soon as I was converted, I started sharing the Word of God, which led many people to call me an evangelist. In fact, I loved making people understand what the Bible said and how it could impact our lives. I've always loved sharing with people what I'm passionate about.

Not only does God have a specific plan for you, but He's given you everything you need to carry it out from the start.

---

[7] Jeremiah 1 : 5

I became a sailing and scuba-diving instructor, a leader trainer, a camp director... then an FLE (French as a Foreign Language) trainer, etc., and everyone agrees that I'm good at teaching.

In 1991, when we were in Bible school, a visiting prophetic ministry gave me a word about what God was calling me to do: Teach the Lord's word of faith and grace, and raise up an army among His people.

5 years later, I met this ministry again at a conference. We didn't know each other and hadn't seen one another since school, but when he began prophesying for me again, he began by repeating the last sentence of the prophecy given at Bible school 5 years earlier.

To this day, my ministry is based on the gifts God gave me from my mother's womb and the themes that ministry prophesied. I delight in teaching, through my books, in Bible schools, in my relationships with the Christians I come into contact with, in the French courses I give or through any other means.

Has my ministry evolved? Of course it has! But over the years, I've seen this common thread running through the choices we make for our ministry and our family.

God is the same eternally; He doesn't vary, He doesn't repent of His callings, and He perseveres until you enter your destiny.

If God sometimes asks us to take a 180° turn, it's often because we were wrong in the first place. But when it happens all the time, it's because we have a problem discerning exactly what God is telling us. Or it could be that we're just getting our own way, while trying to put a divine stamp on everything we do.

Opportunities:

"Hey, could you do something for me…"

On the other hand, I've often seen people who, under the pretext of not having heard God clearly point them in the right direction, do... nothing! You see, I'm so afraid of making a mistake, of doing something that isn't God's plan for me!

The problem with this reasoning is that it leads to immobility.

One day, my pastor called me at 9 pm. We'd had an argument a few days before, and I thought he was coming back at me. In fact, he needed a favor. His children were arriving in Valence too late to catch the last train to Chambéry, and he had some obligations early the next day, so he asked me if I could pick them up. I had to leave around 10 a.m. and wouldn't be back until 2 a.m.!

Clearly, I didn't want to please him, nor did I want to go to bed at 2 am. But I knew it was the right thing to do. So I said yes. I got dressed and drove 4 hours 30 minutes in the middle of the night.

I wasn't expecting anything in particular, I hadn't received any instructions from God to do so, in fact, I hadn't even asked myself the question.

It was just a good deed and didn't need a revelation!

I'm from a generation that learned to drive in cars that weren't equipped with power steering. I can't even tell you what it was like to have to parallel park! The first time I had to do one, I had to gain an inch around my biceps!

And then the driving instructor explained to me that if I clutched the clutch gently and the car started to move forward, the steering would be much lighter and I wouldn't have to make weight-lifting sessions out of my maneuvers!

I've been using this story ever since to tell people that if they want to be led by God in their lives, they need to get moving.

The Bible speaks of this principle on several occasions. First of all, it recommends that we should: "Whatever your hand finds to do with your strength, do it; for there is no work or thought or knowledge or wisdom in Sheol, where you are going".

In other words, when you're dead, it'll be too late for that! So do good while you can.

I was sharing this with a friend who told me that it was an Old Testament principle that couldn't necessarily be transposed to the New Testament, since today we all have the Spirit of God within us. However, I believe that the Holy Spirit within us makes this verse from Ecclesiastes even more topical.

If a good thing comes along, then we should do it. And if for some reason that thing isn't as good as it seems, then the Holy Spirit in me will warn me.

This is exactly the principle that got Paul to move on his missionary journeys as a rule.

Let's read together this passage, which is very instructive as to how Paul was led.

"Timothy was well thought of by the believers in Lystra and Iconium, so Paul wanted him to join them on their journey. In deference to the Jews of the area, he arranged for Timothy to be circumcised before they left, for everyone knew that his father was a Greek. Then they went from town to town, instructing the believers to follow the decisions made by the apostles and elders in Jerusalem. So the churches were strengthened in their faith and grew larger every day.

Next Paul and Silas traveled through the area of Phrygia and Galatia, because the Holy Spirit had prevented them from preaching the word in the province of Asia at that time. Then coming to the borders of Mysia, they headed north for the province of Bithynia, but again the Spirit of Jesus did not allow them to go there. So instead, they went on through Mysia to the seaport of Troas.

That night Paul had a vision: A man from Macedonia in northern Greece was standing there, pleading with him, 'Come over to Macedonia and help us!' So we decided to leave for Macedonia at once, having concluded that God was calling us to preach the Good News there. ".[8]

TO WANT.

Paul wanted to take him with him. In other words, Paul wanted Timothy to be part of his team. It doesn't say that he received it from God.

So he acted on an "urge". And since his "urge" involved complications to his missionary work, had him circumcised for the sake of the Jews...

---

[8] Acts 16 : 3-10

I confess I've never had the courage to operate solely on "an urge" and ask people to be circumcised to accompany me because I "feel" like working with them! But we can see from this story that our desires are not systematically opposed to God's will.

The problem stems from a verse taken out of context, which has manipulated generations of Christians.

"The sinful nature wants to do evil, which is just the opposite of what the Spirit wants. And the Spirit gives us desires that are the opposite of what the sinful nature desires. These two forces are constantly fighting each other, so you are not free to carry out your good intentions. ". [9]

While it's true that the flesh has desires contrary to those of the Spirit, not all our desires arise from it. In the subconscious, flesh and desires are so closely linked that we no longer know how to distinguish between them. Read on:

- *"The fears of the wicked will be fulfilled; the desires of the godly will be granted.".* [10]
- *"I ask the Lord for one thing, which I long for: I would like to dwell in the house of the Lord all my life."* [11]
- *"Delight yourself in the Lord, and he will give you what your heart desires".* [12]
- *"For I desire to see you, to communicate to you some spiritual gift, so that you may be strengthened"*[13].

---

[9] Galatians 5:17

[10] Proverbs 10:24

[11] Psalm 27: 4

[12] Psalm 37: 4

[13] Romans 1:11

TO SUBMIT

We then see that Paul was also led by decisions made by others to whom he submitted when they communicated to the brothers the decisions made by the apostles and the leaders of the Jerusalem Church...

Submitting to directives given by people acting within their sphere of authority is an integral part of being led by the Spirit.

I'm not talking here about obeying everything people in authority say. Again, the Holy Spirit within us must give His approval, but at a priori, [?] we must submit to the people God has placed in positions of authority in a given area.

I remember a praise and worship meeting in the congregation I pastored. In a special moment when the heavens were seemingly opening, I asked everyone to stand up and welcome the Lord as He made His triumphant entry into our midst.

One of the church elders, seated in the front row, decided to remain seated. What's more, he was carrying a sullen posture, arms folded and looking down at me. At that very moment I, and many others with me, felt the Spirit leave our meeting.

At the end of the service, I decided to discuss this with this Elder.

- Why did you have this attitude?

- Because I wasn't told by the Lord to stand up. You're always saying that in worship, we can stand up, sit down, bow down, that it's up to us. So I just sat there.

- Yes, that's what I usually say, but here we had a specific directive from the Holy Spirit.

- I didn't receive it.

This Elder, in general, had a lot of respect for me. He considered me his pastor and supported me in my work, but he was mistaken.

He thought that following a directive in worship without having received it personally was not being led by the Spirit, but by a man. His attitude had created division and grieved the Spirit of God.

When we decide to take part in a common action of any kind - worship, evangelism, restoration of a building... we must accept to submit to the person God has placed in authority in this context.

This is not blind, total submission. If the thing asked of you goes against your deepest conviction, if it takes you down an unacceptable path, etc., then don't submit to it, and leave the place.

But getting up to welcome Jesus doesn't fall into this category...

STOPPED BY THE SPIRIT

... because the Holy Spirit had stopped them from proclaiming the Word...

God is love, and he won't let his children go to the wall, and even less let them crash into it! It took me a long time, too long perhaps, to understand this.

I remember the days of "new wine", when other leaders and I tried to understand and explain the phenomenon. Was it from God? What if it was occult? How could we manage it?

The man in charge of the work at the time told us something very true: "We sincerely love God, and if we put ourselves in danger out of ignorance, God will protect us and get us out of it. I'd rather have fire come down on the church, even if it means having to take the chance of some fire burning out the curtains, than live in a church without fire".

As we shall see later, Paul took risks that were sometimes unconsidered. But God knew his heart, and when the missionary team made a mistake, the Holy Spirit prevented them from going too far.

"Indeed, he who watches over Israel never slumbers or sleeps.

The LORD himself watches over you!

The LORD stands beside you as your protective shade.

The sun will not harm you by day, nor the moon at night.

The LORD keeps you from all harm and watches over your life.

The LORD keeps watch over you as you come and go, both now and forever. ". [14]

Clearly, the desire of Paul and his companions was to serve the Father in whatever He asked of them. Nothing was more important to them than doing "His" will. They were driven by the same desire as Christ Himself. "O Father, if thou wilt, remove this cup from me! But not my will, but yours be done."

---

[14] Psalm 121 : 4-8

This is the key to a Spirit-led life. To really want it. If your desire is to do only the Father's will, you can undertake any good work, and He will help or hinder you according to His plan.

This doesn't mean that you shouldn't seek God's will before setting out, or that sometimes a revelation comes along telling you the right thing to do.

And sometimes revelations:

"… the Lord, accomplishes nothing without first revealing his plans to his servants, the prophets."[15]

Receiving a visitation

... Following Paul's vision, we immediately set our sights on Macedonia.

Clearly, God isn't just going to redirect you every time you head off in the wrong direction. As we see in the story of Paul and his team, He's going to reveal Himself in supernatural ways to those who want to serve Him with a true heart.

Indeed, there are times when we can say, "God told me, or God showed me".

To want to live our Christianity without revelation would be like driving at random along unknown country roads, relying solely on our instincts to find our destination. You might get there, but you might be late; very late!

I, however, don't want to be late for God's plan.

---

[15] Amos 3 : 7

Another thing to note in this story is that Paul's team didn't hesitate to set out on someone else's vision. They trusted him and knew that Paul was in his sphere of authority.

So they set out with him…

A vision for the Mediterranean

A few weeks before we left Toulon for Israel, we were invited to preach at a church in Marseille. During the worship time, a verse began to fill my thoughts. "The first shall be last...".

I wondered if God wanted me to change the message I had planned to share. This often happens to me at the last minute, but that day it wasn't the case. So at the end of the worship time, I preached my message and then made a altar call to pray for the people. As I was praying for a young woman who shared with me that she felt called to be a missionary in Monaco, I had an overwhelming vision.

It was as if I'd been transported in front of the giant screen of those 3D IMAX theaters, on which I saw horrifying scenes. Migrants drowning by the hundreds because of the wickedness of traffickers and the posturing of countries that might welcome them. Prostitution and drugs on the shores of the Mediterranean, the radical Islam of ISIS in Syria murdering thousands of innocents, Greece torn apart by Mammon creating unprecedented poverty, the religious spirit mixed with Freemasonry and superstition overwhelming people... all this passed before my eyes as I heard again and again: *"The first shall be last..."*

Suddenly calm descended and the images disappeared. I could see the Mediterranean from above, and the Lord said to me: "The first shall be last, the Mediterranean basin was the first place of the expansion of my Kingdom, but it has become the most sealed place there is. Satan is on the rampage there, positioning his troops, because he knows that the great awakening is coming. As the Mediterranean was the first, so it will be the last. And at the peak of this awakening, my household will finally say: blessed is he who comes from the Lord...

I want you to open a spiritual path for me across the Mediterranean, from France to Israel".

Well, that's where I lost you, isn't it? You're probably thinking I'm delirious, hallucinating or lying. Or maybe you're thinking that God is the same, yesterday, today and forever.

God didn't stop speaking, as some claim, the day the whole Bible was written. Nor did He decide to stop respecting his commitment to accompany with signs, wonders, speaking in tongues, prophecies, words of wisdom and knowledge... all those who believed! On the contrary, as the number of believers increases, more and more people are able to manifest these things.

So no! I don't need an angel's visitation to set me on my way to serve God (although sometimes...), but for certain things that go beyond our personal framework, we do need such a visitation.

At every major turning point in my life, God has visited me in a supernatural way.

Take my conversion, for example. I was lying in my bedroom in New Zealand when I felt a horrible presence beside me. Some kind of monster seemed to be lurking there in the dark, ready to pounce on me. It was so real that, like a frightened child, I hid my head under the sheets! But then I realized that this presence was with me in bed, and for good reason: this horrible thing was me! I felt so dirty, so damaged, so empty. Where had my beautiful self-righteousness gone? I was then filled with such anguish that I cried out to God:

"Listen! I don't know if you exist, I don't know if your name is really Jesus, but if everything they say about you is true, do something for me right now!"

I was flooded with a peace I'd never known before, all traces of anguish were gone, and the emptiness I'd just experienced deep inside me was filled with a kind of enthusiasm for life.

A year later, when I was baptized in the Holy Spirit. It all began with a burning need (an intuition) to visit some friends who lived in the mountains fifteen miles from my home town. It was two o'clock in the afternoon and I set off by "hitchhiking", after warning them of my arrival. On the outskirts of town, as I held out my thumb to the oncoming car, I heard a voice telling me to walk and pray. The first thing that came to mind was the heat of that early spring and the fifteen miles that separated me from my friends, when suddenly I wondered who had just spoken to me! I started walking, realizing that something special was happening. I prayed as I walked along the side of the road, not feeling the least bit tired. The further I walked, the more I felt God's presence, and the longer I walked. I really felt as if I were sharing my heart with God as I would with an attentive friend.

When I reached the pass in the mountain, I suddenly had to stop.

The setting sun blazed across the horizon, but a greater fire burned within me. I could feel God close by. This incredible experience lasted about ten minutes, and then I heard the voice say to me again: "Go!

A year later, I decided to serve God. It was then that, for the first time in my life, I had a dream inspired by the Holy Spirit.

I was on one of those vast plains in the USA, the sun setting in the distance like on a movie poster. I was surrounded by a crowd of people who cheered and carried me in triumph, because I was going to die for them.

Amidst chants of victory, we marched towards a huge scaffolding of some kind, several hundred feet high and rising incongruously into the sky in such a landscape. I suddenly realized that this was the tool of my imminent death, and I was slightly distressed.

But the singing around me and the confidence of all these people soon dispelled this feeling. Soon we arrived at the foot of the building, which was made of metal tubes and wooden planks with a spiral staircase leading up between. Of the thousands of people accompanying me, a hundred or so began to climb the steps with me, while the others continued to sing and cheer.

We quickly reached the first level. The songs of the crowd reached up to us, and I felt a certain pride in the cheering. After a while, I started climbing towards the top again, but as the scaffolding narrowed, there were only about fifteen of us left.

Gradually, as we climbed higher, the noise of the crowd faded. By the time we reached the second platform, we could hear nothing. Some of those who had accompanied me were already starting to descend. The others at my side gave me one last encouragement before leaving too, and I resumed my ascent, alone. After the first few steps, a doubt assailed me! I turned around, but no one was there. I was alone now, walking towards my own death. But why all this; why should I die for these people I didn't even know? Every step brought a flood of anxiety, and every step seemed like a mountain. An agonizing fear overcame me, I began to cry, then to scream... and I woke up in a sweat!

I immediately understood that what I had just experienced was, in a figurative way, the very beginning of Christ's passion. Just a few minutes of some twenty hours of that passion. I began to grasp the price Jesus had willingly agreed to pay for me.

This supernatural experience made me realize that my life would never belong to me again - He had paid handsomely for it to be His!

It was the same when He sent me on mission to Madagascar, then to Reunion Island. It was then that He asked me to reform my approach to the ministry He had entrusted to me.

So no, I don't hear God speak to me so directly every day. In fact, I tend to be suspicious of people who boast that they have a "chat" with the Lord every morning, and have a mouthful of "God told me".

But I'm sure you'll agree that it would be impossible for me to believe that God has decided to stop speaking, given that we have the King James Bible at our disposal!

“The grand voyage”

From stuggles in storms.

“It is totally irresponsible to proclaim the victory of Christ, as so many Christians do, rather like a mantra, a principle of autosuggestion, as if everything will be done on its own, without going through a battle of faith. We don’t simply win because we are Christians or baptised in the Holy Spirit, but in the measure that we learn to use the weapons of God.”[16]

When I read this in a post of my friend, Claude Payan, I smiled, thinking how many times this is true and should be taught systematically in churches.

How many times have I heard people explaining that with Jesus, everything will be sorted out as if by magic? And that ending our prayers with “in Jesus’ name”, a sort of “Christian Abracadabra” will guarantee us victory, happiness and prosperity! I know this last sentence will bring many Christians to mind. “How dare he? What right does he have to compare the holy name of Jesus with a magical formula?” they will say!

---

[16] Claude Payan in the series “Oui, mais... Il le permet” Résister à l’accusateur! (“Yes, but... He is allowing it”. Resisting the accuser!) Facebook by CJP Exhortation May 2022

It's exactly what the evangelical world has often done!

I have seen this name used so often like an end of prayer piece of punctuation…in Jesus' name, amen! In other words, "I've finished. Next."

Sometimes, it's like a mantra (Jesus, Jesus, Jesus…) as if something in those 5 letters has a magical power. Abracadabra and all will be well…

If we saw an impressive number of miracles in the months that followed buying the yacht with everything seeming to run on greased tracks until the day we were to set sail for Corsica, the battle began the moment we hoisted the sails!

The first crossing between Toulon and Corsica was a dream. Cathy, alas, was not very well, so I was the one who was at the helm, moving the boat onwards bit by bit. I arrived, exhausted, certainly, but happy. I had not lost my navigator's reflexes! During the night crossing, I saw myself again, 30 years younger, crossing the South Pacific towards my encounter with the Lord.

What I had offered to the Lord as a sacrifice 23 years earlier in order to serve Him, He was giving back to me as He had promised! And since "*No trouble is added to the blessing of the Lord*"[17], what could go wrong?

---

[17] Proverbs 10:22

Well, an engine breaking down when we had barely arrived in Corsica, weathering a really demonic storm (I will speak about this further on) that had us stuck in Sardinia for several months, then losing our boat's mast a few months later just as we were leaving!

And I'm not even mentioning people who thought we were backward because, "You see, my dear, they have returned to the old way of living…" or "I *told* you it couldn't be God; look how much they are struggling"!

Such reasoning implies that neither Peter nor Paul nor the other apostles were in God's will, since their "struggles" led them, as thousands of other Christians after them, to prison and death.

Fortunately, many others did not share this attitude and saw beyond the flesh, to the plan that God had.

Christ Himself warned us: *"Do not suppose that I have come to bring peace to the earth. I did not come to bring peace, but a sword. For I have come to turn 'a man against his father, a daughter against her mother, a daughter-in-law against her mother-in-law – a man's enemies will be the members of his own household.'…Then you will be handed over to be persecuted and put to death, and you will be hated by all nations because of me."*[18]

[18] Matthew 10:34-37/24:9-10

"A vaincre sans peril, on triomphe sans gloire".[4] *(A victory without danger is a triumph without glory)!* [19]

Yes, who does not know Sénèque's quote today, which has become a popular proverb.

Indeed, there can be no victory without a battle and when you come to Christ, He does not promise you a world of "Teddy bear kisses, but especially those of GI-Joe"!

[19] Le Cid: Pierre Corneille

The devil in the storm

Let me tell you about one of the worst moments of our trip from France to Israel on our sailboat "Indeed", when we were caught in the worst storm I've ever seen.

While the marine weather forecast predicted a light north-easterly wind, perfect for our crossing to Sicily from Sardinia, after 3 hours of sailing we were hit by a Beaufort force 8/9 storm.

Within minutes, the wind had torn our Gib sail. We were forced to turn back towards the nearest port, Porto di Cala Gonone, about ten nautical miles away.

The danger was great and we immediately called our intercessors in France, Italy and the USA to pray for us.

After an hour, the wind had picked up even more.

Our autopilot was unable to keep us on course in such a storm, so I sent Cathy to safety inside and steered by hand myself, tied up in the cockpit for several hours. Wave after wave broke over the boat, and at times I had to put my hand in front of my face to breathe without swallowing too much water!

[page number?]

Our engine, which was new, following the breakage of our old one in Corsica, was running at full throttle, yet the storm was such that it sometimes pushed us backwards!

The most incredible thing was that if I tried to move away from the direction of the wind, it would change direction to face me again, as if it had a will of its own and had decided to finish us off!

It took us over 6 hours to finally approach the coast and see the lights of the fishermen's village where we wanted to take shelter.

It was nearly eleven o'clock in the evening, the night was inky, and we approached the harbor entrance. But suddenly I was completely lost.

With all the lights from restaurants, bars, neon lights of every color, it was impossible to find the red and green lighthouses that usually mark harbor entrances.

The waves were 10 feet high and I could hear them crashing against the rocks pier, which I unfortunately couldn't see, dazzled by all the city lights.

At the time, I thought we were going to smash on the rocks and that our last hour had come, while less than a few hundred meters away, people were having fun, eating and laughing in the harbor's bars and restaurants.

It was as if Satan, in the guise of a witch, was laughing at us in the middle of the storm.

I began to sail along the beach I'd spotted on the map, telling myself it was better to be stranded on the sand than on the rocks, when suddenly, against the black background of the sky out to sea, I saw a small green light flashing.

I'd finally spotted the harbor entrance. I headed into the channel and spotted two youngsters waving at us from a dock. Ten minutes later, we were moored and safe.

Our friend Ciro, whom we had left a few hours earlier, had come all the way. He was waiting for us on the pier in his 4 × 4 Toyota, and later explained that under the gusts of wind, the car was shaking like a leaf in Fall.

The next day, when we went to the harbor master's office, people told us they'd never seen such a storm. They wondered how we had managed to get into the harbor... The marine meteorological center described the storm as "a very localized, spontaneous hurricane. Less than 15 kilometers in diameter". An inexplicable and unpredictable phenomenon in their view...

I personally believe I have an explanation, however irrational, but very real. We had just escaped a spiritual assault, thanks to the prayerful mobilization of all our intercessors.

The Lord has plans for our peace, but what is His peace?

As we have seen, Jesus teaches us that He came to bring us not peace, but the sword. Yet, later on, doesn't He promise us peace?

"I leave you peace, I give you my peace. I do not give it to you as the world gives. Let not your heart be troubled or alarmed"[20].

At first glance, these texts seem to contradict each other, as do a number of other texts, but this is only true if we take these verses in isolation, whereas the Bible must be understood as a whole.

[20] John 14 : 27

In fact, God promises us peace, and only plans peace for us.

Could there have been a more peaceful place than the Garden of Eden when Adam and Eve had not succumbed to temptation? God's perfect plan for man is that he should live in peace.

But this does not mean, as we so often believe, that enemies no longer exist.

In the Garden of Eden, Adam and Eve lived in peace, despite the presence of Satan. And this lasted until they were defeated by temptation. Then they lost their peace and experienced fear for the first time.

So we can see that the peace God offers us is not the absence of enemies or fighting, but victory! We are at peace when the enemy retreats, because we are victorious.

"Submit yourselves to God; resist the devil, and he will flee from you.".[21]

Consider that by submitting to God and fighting (i.e. resisting the devil), we have victory and therefore the peace of Christ becomes our portion.

There can be no victory without struggle. We must agree to abandon the relative peace of this world, which is merely the nonchalance in which Satan tries to keep us, whereas victory is for the one who resists him!

---

[21] James 4 : 7

Too many lights...
Kill the Light!

Being led by the Spirit and walking by the Spirit are two different things!

As I retraced the story of that storm, I was still filled with the emotional impact of those memories. But it wasn't to make you tremble at our adventures that I wrote the previous chapter.

Cathy and I have been experiencing a spiritual storm in our souls for some months now, and some time before returning to France, during a prayer watch in Gozo, I suddenly recalled in my mind's eye our arrival in a small Sardinian port.

We had had a time of fasting and prayer, and on the first day I had heard God say to me: "Don't look for answers; look for my presence".

It was hard not to look for prophetic answers when our hearts were full of questions, and when our future seemed to depend on the answers to those questions.

But in our search for answers, we sometimes (often?) open our hearts to all kinds of prophetic words, but which may not be inspired by God's Spirit.

It's what I'd call the "moth syndrome": we get closer to the brightest lights, we want to see more clearly, and sometimes we burn our wings...

For example, lately I've seen many people looking for "prophetic" words about events such as Covid, the American elections, the wars and noise of wars, and for their everyday lives. As soon as they received a word, they publicized it on their Facebook, WhatsApp and other social networks, only to end up practically in depression when the opposite of these revelations happened. Sometimes, no sooner had they recovered from their emotions than they were off on the hunt for the next prophecy to share on social networks.

I'm always skeptical when a "prophet" offers a new prophecy to explain why the last one he gave didn't come true.

Worse still, is when he tells us that what God was going to do didn't happen because of cheating by men inspired by the Devil. In other words, God's plan was thwarted because the Devil was stronger.

Doesn't the Father tell us that we will recognize true prophets by the fact that their words come true? ?[22]

I don't believe that God is thwarted in his plans by the devil! The proof is in the resurrection!

Rather, the problem is that some "prophets", as in Jeremiah's day, prophesy in the flesh and, rather than repenting when it becomes obvious that they were off the mark, look for absurd explanations!

The "moth syndrome" means looking for a shortcut to a prophecy rather than taking the trouble to "walk by the spirit". But what does it mean to walk in the spirit?

In a Google search, I found this kind of definition: "Walking by the Spirit would mean leading your life

[22] Jeremiah 28 : 9.

under the guidance of the Holy Spirit, listening to Him, letting Him control everything and above all obeying Him".

This kind of definition, I confess, doesn't entirely satisfy me. I'm convinced that "walking by the spirit" refers directly to our own spirit.

Indeed, if we were to walk under the diktat of the Holy Spirit, that would make us puppets in God's hands. It would have been better if God had started in the Garden of Eden! Then He would have been in control, and His Son and mankind would have been spared much suffering. But God never wanted that.

From the very first chapters of the Bible, we can see that the Lord is a God of relationships. As He contemplates man, He realizes that the humans cannot stand alone. None of the beings He has presented to Him seem compatible with human beings. [meaning?]

God does not consider the question of solitude for the rest of His creation, but only for human, because he is created in His image, and therefore has needs similar to those of his Creator.

God is therefore going to give Adam a being who will be compatible with him, because of the same nature, who will be his counterpart.

In so doing, He established the first institution to govern human relations: marriage.

It is a principle of covenant, between two people of the same nature, different but compatible, just as He will establish covenants with Adam, Noah, Abraham, Isaac, etc., and with each of us in Christ.

Covenant with beings who are compatible with Him.

What creates this compatibility? The spirit that God has given to human beings, and only to them, in the whole of creation. Without it, we would be incompatible with a covenant with God.

He created us in His image, sharing His Spirit with us. Since He's not a puppet, under external control, we can't be either! He wanted and still wants us to collaborate, to walk humbly alongside him, not to be "his things"![23]

In His image, we have been created "Trinitarian". We are body, soul and spirit. If our body is rather easy to identify: it's everything in us that's physical, our soul is less obvious.

Simply put, it's everything in us that isn't physical, but isn't spiritual either. So we'd say our emotions, our culture, our memories, the education we've received, and so on.

Finally, our spirit is that which has been given to us and which no other creature has received: Divine Breath.

This is the spirit that died in every human being with sin[24] and comes back to life when we are born again.

Of course, the fact that it's dead doesn't mean it's no longer there in the human being. It's only inactive, deprived of connection with God, and sometimes can be in connection with an evil spirit, but that's another subject.

From the very beginning, our being is designed to be led by our spirit, which is in turn connected to the "Ruah HaKodesh", the Spirit of God.

---

[23] Micah 6 : 8

[24] Genesis 2-17

This order was to enable our soul and body to thrive under the aegis – backing, support - of our God-driven spirit.

Unfortunately, when the spirit died, due to original sin, our soul took over. It was our soul that Satan addressed when he spoke to Eve. It's your soul that he addresses when he comes to tempt you.

Our soul, the seat of our emotions and all the lies of our upbringing, can be manipulated at will. It reacts much more than it acts, and is always on the lookout for the lost heaven. It constantly seeks to recreate it by its own means, without ever succeeding.

Today, our faith in Christ has enabled our spirit to live again, and Paul invites us to re-establish its authority in our being.

"So this is what I say: walk by the spirit and you will not fulfill the desires of your own nature. For human nature has desires contrary to those of the spirit, and the spirit has desires contrary to those of human nature. They are opposed to each other, so you cannot do what you would like to do. However, if you are led by the spirit, you are not under the law. ".[25]

It's particularly interesting to note that if our spirit truly has authority over our life, Paul tells us that we are then no longer under the law.

Indeed, the law was given to provide our soul with the safeguards it needs to survive until the spirit regains control. In theory, however, we no longer need it.

---

[25] Galatians 5 : 16-18

If our spirit governs our lives, we're not supposed to let our primal instincts (body) or our inherently unstable emotions (soul) drive our existence.

The problem is that, even when resurrected, our spirit often has difficulty in persuading our soul to let go and impose his authority.

It's obvious that most Christians feed their souls far more than their spirit all day long.

If this weren't the case, we'd potentially already have everything we need to understand and implement God's will!

Of course, prophecies can confirm a point or two, advise us on a strategy, give us a helping hand to overcome, but we can't wait on these divine interventions to walk in the spirit on a daily basis.

It's up to us to ensure that our spirit, by spending more and more time with the Spirit, with the Word (the Son) and with the Father, can learn to lead our lives according to divine plans.

He must know how to care for our soul without submitting to it, and respect our body so that its service to the Kingdom lasts as long as possible.

Only then will we be able to do the Father's perfect will.

When the spirit listens to the Spirit!

That said, God is not stingy with supernatural or natural interventions to guide his children in their daily lives, as long as they take the time to pay attention.

During our journey from Toulon to Israel, we were repeatedly warned by the Holy Spirit to change our route, our departure day, and sometimes even our destination. It was on this trip that Cathy and I got into the habit of praying together every day. We'd been dreaming about it for years, but hadn't succeeded.

Let me tell you about a few of those occasions.

When we left Sardinia, for example, we had planned to head straight for Sicily as quickly as possible. So we sailed quietly down the coast, making final adjustments to our new rig. On arrival in Cagliari, we changed the halyard on the mainsail furler and sorted out a couple of other technical problems. A gale was forecast and we decided to stay for three days.

It was during one of our daily prayer times that the conviction took root in our hearts to sail down to Tunisia. It wasn't the most direct route, as it meant "losing at least a couple of weeks on our schedule", but the stopover in Sardinia had cost us months! So a bit more or a bit less...

Discovering the country where my parents were born could have been an interesting experience if we hadn't arrived in the middle of Ramadan. The atmosphere was sinister, and the marina, brand new and only open for a week, was empty. There were a dozen of us in 800 berths. The city of Bizerte was very beautiful, but under a spiritual and military cloud because of the terrorist attacks. What had we come here for?

However, three days later, as we passed Good Cape in the northeast of the country, the Holy Spirit took hold of us in a very special way. As we praised God and interceded for Africa, I saw myself flying in the spirit over the entire continent as far as the Cape of Good Hope. Above each country, I prophesied for the nation, and in the end I had the feeling that God was connecting me with the Cape region of South Africa.

You're going to say, "Another delusion! But a year later, I met some South Africans with whom we became friends. We visited them twice in their homes, and they visited us several times in Gozo.

During a stay with them, I met one of the leaders of their church who shared with me that two years earlier, as we were passing through Tunisia, she had had a vision similar to mine, but she was flying north over South Africa!

Did we meet in spirit? One thing's for sure, these friends made the creation of the Gozo House of Prayer possible through their generosity.

We see in this case something that, through obedience to a rather ordinary point of view, opens the door to a spiritual encounter that has impacted our ministry for several years. God regularly gives us, all of us, such directives, setting His blessing in motion in our lives. We just have to recognize them when we're encountering them.

A little later in our trip, near Athens in Greece, we had planned our route across the Aegean Sea. We had chosen what the locals call the Northern Route. All the stages, island by island, were programmed, and we thought we'd be able to reach Rhodes in around ten days, despite the uncertain weather. Indeed, in summer, the area is swept by the 'Meltem', a violent wind that forces even the biggest cargo ships to take shelter.

We had therefore decided to leave in the evening at around 6 o'clock, when the Meltem would have weakened, in order to reach the next stage in 24 hours before a strong gale was forecast.

I had prepared the boat for this journey, we had done some shopping at the supermarket, the fuel and water tanks were full, and all we had to do was pray for our next trip.

During our prayer time, Cathy and I were told not to leave that day. No specific reason, just a sort of conviction not to go.

So we decided to wait.

That evening, we enjoyed an aperitif on a charter boat that had set up next to us. Its skipper had been sailing these waters for over ten years, so I told him our itinerary.

Don't take the northern route," he said. "You're heading for a storm!"

And he showed us another way and the island where we could take shelter two days later to avoid the forecast gale.

Happy with his advice, which we followed, we spent several days on Kitnos, a magnificent island.

On the second morning, we saw a boat much bigger than ours arrive in a sorry state. Following the northern route, they had spent 36 hours in the storm. It had been impossible for them to get to the island where we had also planned to stay, because the sea was so rough! They told us how, in desperation, they had had to flee south to reach Kitnos, exhausted.

As we listened to their story, we realized how much God had preserved us.

A few weeks later, a similar thing happened to us in Rhodes. We had finally left the Meltem area and were going to follow the Turkish coast all the way to Cyprus. We were looking forward to the next two weeks. Simple, comfortable sailing, friendly people on one of the most beautiful coasts in the Mediterranean – almost a vacation!

The evening before departure, the Holy Spirit clearly told us not to go to Turkey! As I turned a deaf ear, He had to use two other people to convince me. In the morning, I received a call from a brother in France who told me that he too had felt that we shouldn't go to Turkey. Then a message from GHOP in Gibraltar. That morning, during the prayer watch, a sister had prophesied that we shouldn't touch the Turkish coast.

So we finally decided to follow this seemingly pressing directive. We looked for a stopover, and the only possibility was to stop off on a Greek island called Castellorizo, less than 2 nautical miles from the Turkish coast, but outside it all the same.

Two things followed from this obedience.

Firstly, on this island we met an Israeli boat whose occupants we befriended. The skipper, Avi, was a blessing to us when we arrived in Israel, and enabled us to give our testimony to dozens of people in the Haifa marina. It's also thanks to him that we were able to leave the boat there for

6 months, even though we were originally only allowed to stay for 5 days!

But beyond that, our obedience enabled us to avoid the worst. Turkey experienced an attempted coup d'état 2 weeks before we were due to visit. This triggered a persecution of Christians, including the arrest of several pastors and missionaries, accused by the government of being spies in the pay of the USA, who were suspected of supporting the putschists. An American missionary was imprisoned for several months and his wife expelled manu militari the week we were due to sail to Turkey.

Wanting to do His will…

"They passed through Phrygian Galatia because the Holy Spirit had prevented them from proclaiming the Word in the province of Asia. When they reached Mysia, they intended to go to Bithynia, but here again the Spirit of Jesus opposed their plan".

As we saw earlier in the book of Acts, the Holy Spirit will prevent us from getting into dangerous or nasty situations if we take the time to look out for Him.

Our attitude of heart, our sincerity when we declare we want to do His will, and therefore our obedience, will make all the difference between living our life led by our soul or walking in the spirit.

He is the One who searches the heart, who separates the marrow from the bone[26]. *"Indeed, the word of God (Jesus) is living and effective, sharper than any two-edged sword, penetrating to the point of separating soul and spirit, joints and marrow; it judges the feelings and thoughts of the heart.."*[27]

We can't fool Him about our true motives. He will help us if and only if we truly want to do His will.

Today, many who say they want to serve God are not prepared to pay the price or give up their freedom of

[26] Jeremiah 17 : 10, Romans 8 : 27

[27] Hebrews 4 : 10

decision. It's clear that Christ will never force us to be led by His Holy Spirit if we don't sincerely want to.

For me, it's obvious that we (ministry) have a responsibility in the way we preach the gospel, and then in our day-to-day running of the church.

To be honest, I often feel we've distorted the message in order to make it acceptable and see our congregations grow. Then sometimes we've chosen to add our own little touch of concession in order to keep people with us...

Sometimes, we've emphasized our specific theological beliefs and traditions far more than the message of Christ.

At other times, we've put "water in our wine", as they say, so as not to be seen as a cult by the authorities, or simply by our congregation.

But above all, we have embraced a church system, imposed in the 4th century by a Roman emperor, that had nothing to do with God's plan for His Church.

This emperor, setting up a caste of God's professionals and subjecting people to them, emptied the gospel of its essence.

It was no longer a question of becoming disciples, but of being believers. The sacraments dispensed by the church replaced faith in the One who gives eternal life.

To be saved was to belong to the church.

We no longer needed to hear God speak to us in a personal relationship; all we had to do was listen to the priest, then the pastor...

No more price to pay for the gospel except indulgences, then tithes...

Today's most charismatic churches are not far removed from these principles, even if they deny it. The style may have changed, but the principles remain the same.

Not only has this led to flagrant abuses of authority in the congregations, but worse still, it has produced generations of Christians incapable of hearing God for themselves.

They remain dependent on the leaders of their movement, to whom they owe total submission or face excommunication. I experienced this myself when I refused to put my ministry on hold at the behest of the pastor of an evangelical church when we lived in the USA.

I'm convinced that this is the reason why so many churches are being shipwrecked today, and that without a profound reformation we won't see the glorious Bride that Christ comes to seek.

So let's stop doing things out of habit and carry out a real analysis of how we function as a body, a ministry and a disciple.

Some thoughts on a shipwreck.

While praying one morning in the HOP Gozo, Cathy had shared with me a thought about Paul's shipwreck in Malta. For months we had been praying, praising and interceding every day, sometimes for several hours a day, with times of fasting, but everything seemed to be going from bad to worse.

Then an email arrived: *"Dear Mikaël and dear Cathy, I'm going to pray for you, even if I don't quite understand why you're so keen to stay in Malta in these particular and difficult conditions.*

In any case, I'm praying for you..."

I answered this friend: *"Because God asked us to go to Malta and hasn't yet asked us to leave yet".*

But a question was growing in my heart: were we and our ministry being shipwrecked in Malta?

So I began to study the story of Paul's shipwreck, first in the Bible, but also, since we were in Malta, in history, or at least in local legends.

As I studied this, I realized that this shipwreck had its origins long before that fateful autumn between Crete and Malta. In fact, it takes root at the end of the second voyage when God warns Paul of imminent danger in Jerusalem. I will now share several passages from the Acts of the Apostles recounting these events.

"All I know is that the Holy Spirit is warning me from town to town that I should expect imprisonment and much suffering"...

"There were disciples there. When we found them, we stayed with them for seven days. But they, moved by the Spirit, advised Paul not to go to Jerusalem".

"He came to us, took Paul's belt and used it to bind his hands and feet. This is what the Holy Spirit declares," he said. The man to whom this belt belongs will be bound in this way by the Jews in Jerusalem, and then they will deliver him into the hands of the Gentiles".

"On hearing this statement, we and the believers in Caesarea begged Paul not to go up to Jerusalem. But he replied: "What are you doing there? Do you want to break my heart with your tears? I'm quite prepared not only to go to prison, but even to die in Jerusalem for the Lord Jesus."
As we couldn't get him to change his mind, we stopped insisting and just said: "The Lord's will be done"! [28]

We know the outcome of this story: Paul will be beaten, imprisoned, almost killed several times, and then after two years in prison in Caesarea, he will embark on the sea journey that ends in Malta with a shipwreck.

Was this God's plan? Was there no other way to organize Paul's missionary journey to Rome?

In fact, did Paul make an error in judgment, or was he, perhaps, simply being presumptuous?

Another disturbing fact in Paul's passage to Jerusalem, which led to his arrest:
"After hearing him, they began to celebrate the glory of the Lord. Then they said to him, "You see, brother, how many thousands of Jews there are among the believers, and all of them are zealous for the law. Now they have heard that you teach all Jews living among

[28] Acts 20 :23 to Acts 21 : 12-14

non-Jews to abandon the Law of Moses; you would tell them not to circumcise their children and not to conform to customs. So what should we do? No doubt they'll hear that you've come. So do as we tell you. There are four men among us who have made a vow. Take them with you, perform the purification ceremony with them and provide for their expenses so that they can shave their heads. In this way, everyone will know that what they have heard about you is false, but that you too live by the law. As for believers of non-Jewish origin, we have communicated our decision to them in writing: they must abstain from meat sacrificed to idols, from blood, from strangled animals and from sexual immorality. ".[29]

Was Paul supposed to comply with the church's request, knowing that he himself no longer submitted to the Law of Moses, but rather to its principles?

In so doing, he precipitated the events that would lead to his downfall. We see here a deed that has more to do with the fear of men than the fear of God, or at least the desire to please the Jews of Jerusalem.

We have often idealized, and are sometimes inclined to believe, that everything written about the deeds of these heroes of the faith, the apostles, was God's perfect plan.

I am convinced that this is not the case. The casting of lots for Judas' replacement, for example, seems to me to be a mistake. God had not asked the remaining 11 to choose a replacement for Judas, but to wait for the Holy Spirit to be given to them, in Jerusalem. Matthias was certainly a great guy, but that's no way to be chosen in a lottery!

We have many other examples of this throughout the New Testament. Peter's choices were sometimes

[29] Acts 21 : 20-25

questionable, so much so that Paul had to rebuke him publicly...

Is it therefore possible, in the story of this journey and shipwreck in Malta, that Paul missed the divine plan? Why did he appeal to the emperor when he was about to be released?

"This man has done nothing to deserve death or imprisonment; he could have been released if he hadn't appealed to the emperor".

When I read this, it seems to me to be more a spontaneous (carnal?) reaction than the result of a revelation.

If Paul had been released, wouldn't he have been just as effective, if not far more so, being free in his movements rather than in his chains?

By ignoring the warnings of the prophets on the road to Jerusalem and appealing to the emperor, didn't he place himself under an authority other than that of Christ?

He had indeed been called to preach in Rome, but not necessarily as a prisoner.

Two very similar shipwrecks!

"The sailors were frightened; they each implored their god, and threw the objects on the boat into the sea to lighten it. Jonah had gone down to the bottom of the boat, lay down and slept soundly.

'As we were violently battered by the storm, the next day they threw the cargo into the sea, and on the third day they threw the ship's tackle into the sea with their own hands. ". [30]

The question then is: was Paul's shipwreck due to a spiritual battle to prevent his mission, as some people claim, or was it because God needed to speak to Paul, just as He needed to speak to Jonah?

I've sometimes heard that God brought about this shipwreck so that the people of Malta could be converted. Such dramatic circumstances would mean that what was at stake in the evangelization of Malta was crucial.

The fruit borne would have to be worthy of the adventure! Did it? It would appear not.

No church seems to have been established as an outcome of Paul's three-month stay. No letters from Paul or other apostles to the church in Malta.

---

[30] Jonah 1 : 5 Acts 27 : 18-19

It would even seem that the first Christianization of these islands, apart from the Constantine regime, did not take place until the 11th century, when the Normans took over the archipelago from the Muslims of North Africa.

A census carried out in 1240, one hundred and fifty years after the Norman conquest, by a priest, Abbot Gilbert, counted some 9,000 inhabitants on Malta and Gozo, including 771 Muslim families, 250 Christian families including Muslim converts, and 33 Jewish families. Finally, between 1240 and 1250, Frederick II of the Holy Roman Empire expelled the Muslims, although many "converted" to remain on the islands.

It has to be said that, although Paul healed many of the sick and won the sympathy of the inhabitants of Malta, no church was established there.

The more I study the texts of the book of Acts, the more I believe that Paul got into this dramatic situation of his own making, and that it may have had nothing to do with God's plan, who must have used these circumstances to be able to speak to his servant.

Could it be that Paul was "missing the mark", the very definition of the word sin?

In any case, it's clear that this man of God, like each of us, had "good and bad days"! I think we can say that in these passages from the book of Acts, they were rather 'bad' days!

I'm convinced that his heart desired only God's will, but his actions failed to comply with God's repeated warnings.

A time, times...
& Kairos!

'Sons of Issachar, who knew how to discern the times to understand what Israel should do...."[31]

Among the 12 tribes of Israel, there were people who had received a special gift: discerning the times!

In 1999, on Reunion Island, I organized a conference on this theme. In 2018, in Gozo, it was once again the theme the Lord had given us for our prayer conference.

It seems that God regularly invited me to meditate on this notion of discerning (understanding, apprehending...) the times I was entering or exiting.

"There is a time for everything, a time for everything under heaven...".

Many people talk about God's time.

It would therefore be logical to consider that if God has given some people the ability to discern His times, that He Himself is subject to them, which is obviously not the case since He is eternal.

This concept of eternity is difficult for us to understand, as we live for the moment in a temporary body and thus, we approach time chronologically. This means that we often

[31] 1 Chronicles 12 : 32

confuse eternity with a passing of time (Chronos) which never ends. But actually, eternity is the absence even of this notion of time!

Yesterday, today, tomorrow are words that have no impact on God. He demonstrated this when He declared to Moses:

"I AM WHO I AM." And he said, "Say this to the people of Israel: I AM has sent me to you.".[32]

The same concept was expressed by Jesus himself when he was arrested: *"And when Jesus said to them, 'I AM,' they drew back and fell to the ground"*.

This absence of time (Chronos) means that God constantly has before him all the events that make up human history.

When He asks us to discern the times, what we think of as "prophecy" does not involve a "divinatory ability", but rather the "interface" between God's omniscience and our temporal reality. This is why Old Testament prophets were called "Seers". They saw a portion of eternity; they didn't guess at it!

That's what we do when we walk by the Spirit rather than by the flesh. We are then, like the sons of Issachar, able to discern God's time (Kairos).

K*airos* (καιρός) is a concept which, when combined with *aiôn* (destiny) and with *"chronos"* (time as we understand it), allows us to discern events according to God's eternal dimension.

We could define it as the time of opportunity. It's a special moment when anything is possible. In everyday

[32] Exodus 3 : 14

language, we'd call it a turning point! There's a notion of "before and after".

Kairos enters a dimension of time that has nothing to do with the linear notion of chronos, and could be considered as another divine dimension of time. It opens the door to a different perception of the event, of oneself, but also of God. An immaterial notion of time measured not by the watch, but by the feeling caused by our spirit coming into contact with His Spirit.

Many people want to ignore this notion of "Kairos" in their listening to God. They perceive what God wants to do, but are unable to situate it in their narrow view of time.

So there are words that God gives that are not good to implement or seek out immediately. We see many examples of this throughout the Bible.

Abraham, who, wanting to precipitate the word about his descendants, goes to bed with his servant. Joseph, who shares his dream with his brothers and ends up being sold into slavery. Or, on a more positive note, David, who, after being made king, refuses to dethrone Saul when he has the chance, aware that it's not yet his "time" in God's plan!

All too often, I've seen people who, on receiving a prophetic word, become so obsessed with it that they miss out on all the preparation that must precede its fulfillment. Some have therefore failed to enter into God's plan.

"Jesus answered her, 'Woman, what is there between me and you? My time has not yet come...

Jesus said to them: 'My time has not yet come, but your time is always ready".[33]

[33] John 2 : 4 ; John 7 : 6

As we see here, Jesus himself submitted to God's KAÏROS in his life.

It's time for us to submit to it too. Patience is a fruit of the spirit. We must therefore learn to persevere, even when time seems long.

As I shared at the beginning of this book, it was 20 years between God's promise to give me back my Isaac (a passion for sailing and boats) and the day He actually gave it back to me.

When my children were little, we used to sing this song to them: what God does is perfect in its own time... it's up to us to believe it too!

A renewed mind

If God has decided to renew our mind when He saves us, it's because He expects us to use it. This may seem obvious, and yet...

Regularly throughout the history of the church, we have seen it mistrust the mind, seeking again and again to oppose it to faith.

I remember believing that using my brain, my mind to interpret the Bible was a sin! Until I found myself publishing a brochure by my friend Claude Payan entitled: "How to interpret the Word of God"!

I told my friend: "You don't interpret the Word of God, you obey it!

He explained to me, with great kindness and a little humor, that if God has found it good to renew our mind...

While I've done a lot of crazy things in my life, like giving up my career just when it could finally be fully established, I've always tried not to do anything too stupid.

It's all the same! you might say. Well, no, it's very different.

Not doing stupid things requires us to think, to calculate, to implement strategies, to learn or to surround ourselves with competent people.

Too many people, just because they've been called by God to do something, think they don't need talent or hard work.

If talent is God's gift, given to us when we were still in the womb, and related to our destiny, work is the part that belongs to us. And it usually starts with using our brains!

"For which of you, if he wants to build a tower, does not first sit down to calculate the expense and see if he has enough to finish it, lest, having laid the foundation, he cannot finish it, and all who see him begin to mock him, saying: This man began to build, and could not finish"?[34]

In the Christian world, I've more often seen people do stupid things than do crazy things, under the pretext of walking by faith.

I remember one brother who wrote checks "by faith"! He found himself bankrupt and in debt "by faith"!

Faith isn't supposed to be blind, whatever some people think. On the contrary, it's based on something very concrete. What God declares!

Years ago, my wife and I decided to "live by faith". I don't mind telling you that I've often doubted the wisdom of this expression: "living by faith"!

I'd like to take a closer look at this expression with you. "Living by faith."

Definition of Living: It's the state of being alive, but also the way in which we live, such as procuring the means to live, supporting our loved ones or behaving in a certain way, conforming to customs.

---

[34] Luke 14 : 27-30

Definition of faith: It is the attitude of man that accepts and holds as true realities that are invisible, or uncontrollable. It is an act by which man voluntarily entrusts himself to God, recognizing him as good, faithful and able to keep his promises.

We can therefore define "Living by faith" as follows: "Living our daily lives, in terms of our material needs (body), emotional needs (soul) and spiritual needs (spirit), in conformity with the fact that our God is good, faithful and able to keep all the promises He has given us in the covenant He established with us in Jesus His Son".

From this definition, we can draw a fact that seems to me to be of fundamental importance for the body of Christ.

All of us who are justified by Christ are "righteous" and therefore called to live by faith.

In fact, I believe that walking by the Spirit systematically implies that we live by faith.

For the righteous shall live by his faith![35]

---

[35] Habakkuk 1 :1-5, 2 :1-4

A compass for your journey in God's plan!

"A new commandment I give you, love one another; as I have loved you, so you also should love one another. By this all will know that you are my disciples, if you have love for one another.. "[36]

In this passage, Jesus associates the fact that people see that we are disciples of Christ, and therefore do his will, not with the signs, wonders and healings we might perform, but with the fact that we love one another!

Let's read these verses together to see for ourselves:

'Many will say to me in that day, Lord, Lord, have we not prophesied by your name? Have we not cast out demons in your name? And have we not done many miracles in your name? Then I will say to them openly, I never knew you; depart from me, you who commit iniquity". [37]

All these manifestations of power do not prove that you are followers of Christ, only that God is faithful to his word and full of compassion.

Nor will they necessarily convince people of the gospel you preach.

"Seeing what Paul had done, the crowd raised their voices, and said in the Laconian language, the gods in human form have come down to us. They called Barnabas Jupiter, and Paul Mercury, because he was

[36] John 13 : 34&35 :

[37] Matthew 7: 22& 23

the one who carried the word. The priest of Jupiter, whose temple was at the entrance to the city, brought bulls with bandages to the gates, and wanted, like the crowd, to offer a sacrifice".

The only thing that will truly demonstrate our belonging to Christ in the eyes of the world is the love we are able to show not only towards others, but also towards our enemies.

When Christ tells us: *I give you a new commandment*, He's not talking about a good idea, an option. Nor is it the fruit of an intuition. It's a commandment! We owe this love to one another!

"Owe no one anything, except to love one another; for he who loves another has fulfilled the law.".[38]

When we are in the assembly of brothers, we owe each other love. According to the Bible, you have the right to ask your neighbor to give you this love on Sunday mornings. Just as you have no right to refuse it!

If we want to walk by the spirit, as we keep declaring, we have to stop playing church and become the church.

I love this question a man once asked Jesus:

"Teacher, which is the greatest commandment in the Law? Jesus answered: You shall love the Lord your God with all your heart, with all your soul and with all your mind. This is the first and greatest commandment. And here is the second, which is similar: you shall love your neighbor as yourself. On these two commandments depend all the Law and the Prophets. ".

Using the expression: "*And here is the second, which is similar* " Christ puts on the same level loving God with all

---

[38] Romans 13 : 8

our strength, with all our soul, with all our thoughts, and loving our neighbor!

But who is this famous "neighbor" whom we must love as ourselves? In biblical Hebrew, the root of the word "neighbor" is the verb to see. In this sense, my neighbor is "the one I see". If I see you, you are my neighbor!

So I owe this love to every single person on this earth that I can see!

My friends, we might as well practice loving one another today, because tomorrow, it's the people of the world, the sinners and the torturers of Christians, who will come to claim their due from you!

For Jesus tells us:

"But I say to you, love your enemies, bless those who curse you, do good to those who hate you, and pray for those who mistreat and persecute you..."[39]

I'll always remember the testimony of Corrie Ten Boom, who faced her family's Nazi tormentor, and chose to forgive and love.

She said: "I was frozen, my heart frozen, but forgiveness is a voluntary act, and the will can be exercised, whatever the temperature of the heart.

In a situation like this, we discover whether we are the body of Christ or just playing church.

If we listen to our feelings, we won't be able to love, because we give our soul authority over our life. But the love we are talking about here cannot find its source in our

---

[39] Matthew 5 : 44

feelings, for the good reason that it is not a feeling, but the Fruit of the Spirit.

"However, the fruit of the Spirit is love, joy, peace, patience, kindness, goodness, faithfulness, gentleness and self-control. ".[40]

Our feelings are produced by our soul, whereas this Love is produced by our relationship with God! We will only be able to manifest this kind of love if we are in a truly intimate relationship with the One who enables us to bear this kind of fruit:

"I am the vine, you are the branches. He who abides in me and I in him bears much fruit, for without me you can do nothing. ".[41]

If we want to be able to give this love to the people of the world, we have to make our relationship with God a priority!

But we also need to long for it, just as Paul encourages us to do when he shows us the way par excellence:

"Seek the best gifts. I'll show you the way par excellence. If I speak the tongues of men, and even of angels, but have not love, I am a sounding brass or a clanging cymbal.

If I have the gift of prophecy, the understanding of all mysteries and all knowledge, if I even have all faith to the point of moving mountains, but do not have love, I am nothing.

And if I distribute all my goods to the poor, if I even surrender my body to the flames, but I don't have love, it's of no use to me.

Love is patient, it is full of goodness; love is not envious; love does not boast, it is not puffed up with pride, it does nothing dishonest, it does not seek its own interest, it is not irritated, it does not suspect evil, it

---

[40] Galations 5 : 22

[41] John 15:5

does not rejoice in injustice, but rejoices in the truth; it forgives all things, it believes all things, it hopes all things, it endures all things". [42]

[42] 1 Corinthians 12 : 31 to 13 : 7

Conclusion

Humble and inspired.

"You have been made aware of what your God expects of you".[43]

Knowing what God expects of us should be a priority for every one of His children-servants. It's not enough to be a child, nor is it enough to be a servant. We need to know both who we are and what we need to do if we are to serve God effectively and do His will. To do this, we can't overlook aspiring to the best gifts, as Paul encourages us to do. "Seek love. Aspire also to spiritual gifts..."

This is not only pleasing to God, but necessary for a smooth functioning of the body of Christ and our own lives.

"Aspire" is a very interesting word. It appeals to the physical (breathing) as much as to the spiritual (being inspired by the Spirit)[44].

It's the same notion we find in the fact that God breathed His Spirit into the human being He had just formed, or when Jesus "breathed" on His disciples before sending them.

In the notion of breathing, we see the absolute necessity of aspiration for life.

---

[43] Micah 6 : 8

[44] Greeks call it πνεῦμα, and Latins *spiritus*, i.e. breath, what we call aspiration or inspiration.

So Paul invites us to seek out gifts in the understanding that this is vital to our lives. Being inspired by God is not an "option" for anyone who call himself a Christian.

In conclusion, let's return to this verse from Micah.

"It has been made known to you, O man, what is good and what the Lord requires of you. That you practice justice, love mercy and walk humbly with your God".

From the author
translated to English.

Chased by Your Grace

Translated by Richard Waterhouse

Proof reading McCall Harrison

Passport for worshiping In spirit and in truth

Translated by Rosie Taylor

Passport for a new identity in Christ

Proof reading by Rosie Taylor